WHADDAYA SAY?

WHADDAYA SAY?

Guided Practice
in Relaxed
Spoken English

NINA WEINSTEIN

 PRENTICE HALL REGENTS, Englewood Cliffs, New Jersey 07632

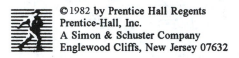©1982 by Prentice Hall Regents
Prentice-Hall, Inc.
A Simon & Schuster Company
Englewood Cliffs, New Jersey 07632

Printed in the United States of America

30 29 28 27 26 25 24 23 22

ISBN: 0-13-951708-1

Illustrated by Don Robb

Cover and page design:
etc. graphics, Canoga Park, CA

Typeset in Eras and Clarendon:
etc. graphics, Canoga Park, CA

Prentice-Hall International (UK) Limited, *London*
Prentice-Hall of Australia Pty. Limited, *Sydney*
Prentice-Hall Canada Inc., *Toronto*
Prentice-Hall Hispanoamericana, S. A., *Mexico*
Prentice-Hall of India Private Limited, *New Delhi*
Prentice-Hall of Japan, Inc., *Tokyo*
Simon & Schuster Asia Pte. Ltd., *Singapore*
Editora Prentice-Hall do Brasil, Ltda., *Rio de Janeiro*

CONTENTS

TO THE STUDENT

You have probably noticed that when Americans speak slowly, clearly, and carefully, they are not too hard to understand. When they speak quickly or in a relaxed, informal way, however, it is often very difficult to know what they have said. This happens because of pronunciation changes. If exactly the same words are spoken in "careful" English and then in "relaxed" English, they will usually sound quite different.

Usually, words spoken with relaxed pronunciation are easier and quicker to say (even if they are hard to understand.) EXAMPLES: "*What do you want to* do?" becomes "**Whaddaya *wanna* do?" and "I *don't know* what I'm *going to* do" becomes "I **donno* what I'm **gonna* do." In this book you will learn about these and other relaxed speech patterns. As you work through the book and listen to its tape, you will learn to recognize these pronunciation changes when you hear them. As a result, your ability to understand spoken English will increase noticeably.

You may want to use some of the examples from this book in your own speech in order to give it a more natural sound. If you do, ask your teacher for help. This is necessary because relaxed speech is not used in all situations. It is not acceptable, for example, at any kind of formal function, or when people must repeat something that was not understood. Relaxed speech is very natural and common, however, when people are talking at informal gatherings or meetings, or when they are making "small talk" with friends.

As you use this book, you will notice that many words and phrases are spelled in an unusual way. These "special spellings" are only intended to give you a general idea of how the relaxed speech examples are pronounced. Do not use these "special spellings" in your own writing. They are not acceptable in written English.

To help you remember that relaxed speech is not appropriate for all situations, and to help you remember that the "special spellings" used in this book are not acceptable in written English, we have put an asterisk (*) in front of each relaxed speech example.

TO THE TEACHER

Generally speaking, ESL students learn to understand their teachers (and the tapes they hear in language lab) without too much difficulty. When they are listening to American friends, clerks and shop-keepers, or "the man on the street," however, this situation often changes dramatically. To a large degree this may be explained by the fact that "classroom English" and "the English of the real world" sound different. The careful, clearly articulated (and often slower) language typically heard in class and the "relaxed speech" so commonly heard outside it do not quite match. When students encounter this phenomenon, therefore, a communications breakdown usually occurs: what they expect to hear and what they actually hear are not the same thing. The result is at best frustration and at worst utter mystification.

If relaxed speech were no more than slang or "sloppy diction" (and thus only characteristic of substandard language usage), there would be little cause for concern. The fact is, however, that it is heard when Americans of almost all backgrounds and educational levels speak quickly or in an informal, casual manner. Students will, therefore, encounter relaxed speech often, and should be prepared to deal with it. *Whaddaya Say?* has been written for just that purpose.

Whaddaya Say? is not intended to teach relaxed speech in and of itself. It is *not* intended to be a pronunciation text. Instead, its goal is to help students understand the relationships between carefully articulated English and its more informal, relaxed counterpart. When these relationships become clear and students learn to recognize them in spoken English, they will have acquired a valuable key to understanding. Consequently, their listening comprehension skills will improve markedly.

THE LESSON MATERIALS

The *Whaddaya Say?* text consists of twenty lessons; accompanying cassettes contain a recording of the aural portions of each lesson. Within the text, each lesson presents a different relaxed speech pattern (or *reduced form*) and reviews previously presented material. All the lessons are divided into three parts.

In *Part One* of each lesson, students are expected to listen only; as they listen, they follow in their books the written representations of what they hear. What they hear is pairs of sentences. Both sentences in each pair contain exactly the same words, but one illustrates carefully articulated pronunciation, while the relaxed speech counterpart is illustrated in the other.

In *Part Two*, students close their books and listen again to the relaxed speech examples that they heard in Part One. This time, however, the sentences in "relaxed" pronunciation are given without their carefully articulated counterparts. The students' task is to "translate" what they hear into careful pronunciation.

In *Part Three*, students open their books and hear a conversation built around the particular relaxed speech pattern treated in the lesson (and also previously presented patterns). At first, they listen only, hearing the conversation with "relaxed" pronunciation. After hearing the conversation at least once, their task is to fill in the blanks in the transcript using the appropriate standard spellings of what they have heard. Each blank or series of blanks corresponds to relaxed speech patterns featured in the conversation. An Answer Key for each conversation is provided at the back of the text.

In *Whaddaya Say?*, relaxed speech patterns are graphically represented by what might be called "special spellings" (*gonna, *wanna, *whaddaya, go *da, etc.). These "special spellings" are intended to show, in a general and easily understood way, the particular pronunciation changes being worked with. Each "special spelling" is preceded by an asterisk to remind students that it is not a correct spelling. Although the pronunciations could, of course, have been indicated with more accuracy by means of phonetic transcriptions, this was decided against so as not to burden students (and teachers!) with a set of symbols that would be esoteric at best. Students are not likely to encounter these "special spellings" (or something similar) in anything but comics or very casual notes; therefore, it should naturally be pointed out that they are inappropriate for the writing the students will be required to do.

Many students will want to adopt relaxed pronunciation into their speech. Point out to them that it is not appropriate for all conversational situations. Provide them with guidance about when the use of relaxed speech is and is not appropriate.

Whaddaya Say? may be used with any student who has contact with spoken American English—university students, students in adult school or private language institutes, students in high school ESL programs, tourists, business people, and so on. The text may also be used at almost all levels of instruction—from beginning to advanced. For best results, students should, of course, be familiar with the vocabulary and grammatical content of any given lesson before attempting to work with it.

The amount of time needed to work through *Whaddaya Say?* or any one of its lessons will depend on many factors, including a student's general English competency, how well the format of the lessons is understood, and how much "real world English" the student has already been exposed to. As a general rule of thumb, each lesson represents *at least* forty-five minutes of presentation and practice material (for a total of *at least* fifteen hours); considerably more time could, however, be necessary.

SUGGESTIONS FOR USE OF THE MATERIALS

1. Introduce each *Whaddaya Say?* lesson to students before allowing them to work on it. Be sure the focus of each lesson, the lesson format, and what students are required to do in each part of the lesson are clearly understood. Be sure students realize that the relaxed speech examples they hear are not appropriate in all situations.

2. At this point have students work through *Part One.* Emphasize that students should listen carefully, paying particular attention to the pronunciation differences in the careful and relaxed renderings of each pair of sentences. Be sure students understand that the meaning of both sentences in a pair is the same, but the "feeling" and situations in which the different renderings would be used are different.

EXPANSION: *Part One* can be expanded by having students listen to (and repeat, if desired) *all* the example sentences with careful pronunciation (that is, the left-hand examples); then the same procedure can be followed for all the relaxed pronunciation (right-hand) examples. For added reinforcement, *Part One* can then be worked through again, following the format of the text.

3. Next have students work through *Part Two.* Be sure that they understand their task: to close their books and listen to the relaxed speech examples from *Part One,* then "translate" what they have heard into careful pronunciation. Spend as much time as is necessary with *Part Two;* students should be able to give spontaneous "translations" into careful pronunciation of the relaxed forms that they hear.

EXPANSION: *Part Two* may be expanded by creating additional sentences modeled on those included in *Whaddaya Say?*. As students hear these additional examples, they respond by giving the careful equivalents.

4. Now go on to *Part Three.* Be sure students understand that they will hear a conversation featuring the relaxed speech elements introduced in any given unit plus other elements from previous units. Also be sure students realize that they are to fill in the blanks with the *conventional spellings* of the reduced forms that they will hear. Emphasize that "special spellings" are *not* to be used.

For optimum results, students should listen to the entire dialog all the way through at least once before attempting to fill in any blanks.

It may also be advisable to stop and/or replay the tape after each line of dialog, since filling in the blanks can be quite challenging. Do *not* stop the tape in the middle of lines or utterances, however, since context is very important.

Once students have filled in all the blanks, play the entire conversation again so students may check their answers. Then either go over the answers with the students, have them hand in their books so you can correct their answers, or have them confirm what they have written by consulting the Answer Key at the back of the text.

EXPANSION: *Part Three* may be expanded by creating more sentences modeled after those heard in the conversation. On hearing such additional examples, students respond by "translating" them into careful pronunciation and conventional spelling.

you ⟶ *ya

NOTE: *You* is not pronounced ***ya** if stressed.

PART I

Listen to the tape. You will hear the pairs of sentences listed below. The first sentence in each pair will be spoken with *careful pronunciation*. The second sentence will be spoken with *relaxed pronunciation*.

CAREFUL (SLOW) PRONUNCIATION

1. Do you need exact change for these machines?
2. Yes, you need two quarters.
3. Do *you* have any change?
4. No, but I need some, too. If you give me a dollar, I'll get some.
5. Here's a dollar. Where do you get the change?
6. You get it at the store next door.
7. Oh. Will you buy me some soap, too? I'll give you some more money.
8. Sure. Will you watch my clothes while I'm gone?
9. Of course. Will you be back soon?
10. Yes, I'll see you in just a few minutes.

RELAXED (FAST) PRONUNCIATION

1. Do *ya need exact change for these machines?
2. Yes, *ya need two quarters.
3. Do *you* have any change?
4. No, but I need some, too. If *ya give me a dollar, I'll get some.
5. Here's a dollar. Where do *ya get the change?
6. *Ya get it at the store next door.
7. Oh. Will *ya buy me some soap, too? I'll give *ya some more money.
8. Sure. Will *ya watch my clothes while I'm gone?
9. Of course. Will *ya be back soon?
10. Yes, I'll see *ya in just a few minutes.

Close your book. Listen to the tape. You will hear the 10 sentences with relaxed pronunciation that you heard in Part I. After you hear each sentence, say the same thing, but use *careful pronunciation*.

PART III

Open your book. Listen to the tape. You will hear a conversation. In it, the speakers will use relaxed pronunciation. As you listen, fill in the blanks with the words you would hear if the speakers were using *careful pronunciation*. Replay the tape as necessary.

AT THE LAUNDROMAT

TONY: "How do _____ work these washing machines?"
(1)

SANDY: "First, _____ put in the clothes. Then _____ put in
(2)   (3)

the soap. Then _____ put in the exact change."
(4)

TONY: "What change do _____ need?"
(5)

SANDY: "_____ need two quarters."
(6)

TONY: "Then what?"

SANDY: "_____ decide what temperature _____ want."
(7)   (8)

TONY: "OK. Then what?"

SANDY: "Then _____ push in the money."
(9)

TONY: "Is that everything _____ do?"
(10)

SANDY: "That's everything. Then _____ just wait until the clothes
(11)

are finished."

TONY: "Thanks. I'm glad _____ came by when _____ did."
(12)   (13)

3

2

What do you
What are you $\longrightarrow$ ***Whaddaya**

NOTE: A related form, ***whadda,** is used when *What do* is followed by either *we* or *they*. Example: "*Whadda we need?", "Whadda they want?"

PART I

Listen to the tape. You will hear the pairs of sentences listed below. The first sentence in each pair will be spoken with *careful pronunciation*. The second sentence will be spoken with *relaxed pronunciation*.

CAREFUL (SLOW) PRONUNCIATION	RELAXED (FAST) PRONUNCIATION
1. What do you want?	1. *Whaddaya want?
2. What do you think?	2. *Whaddaya think?
3. What do we need?	3. *Whadda we need?
4. What are you doing?	4. *Whaddaya doing?
5. What are you thinking?	5. *Whaddaya thinking?
6. What are you watching?	6. *Whaddaya watching?
7. What are you drinking?	7. *Whaddaya drinking?
8. What do they do after work?	8. *Whadda they do after work?
9. What do you do after school?	9. *Whaddaya do after school?
10. What do they think we should do?	10. *Whadda they think we should do?

PART II

Close your book. Listen to the tape. You will hear the 10 sentences with relaxed pronunciation that you heard in Part I. After you hear each sentence, say the same thing, but use *careful pronunciation*.

4

PART III

Open your book. You will hear a conversation. In it, the speakers will use relaxed pronunciation. As you listen, fill in the blanks with the words you would hear if the speakers were using *careful pronunciation*. Replay the tape as necessary.

WEEKEND PLANS

DAVID: "_____ _____ _____ doing this Saturday?"
             (1)   (2)   (3)

TOM: "Nothing special. _____ _____ _____ have in
                                (4)   (5)   (6)

mind?"

5

DAVID: "A big picnic. _____ _____ _____ think?"
       (7)   (8)   (9)

TOM: "It sounds like fun! Who do _____ think we should go
                                    (10)
       with?"

DAVID: "Well, how about Debra, Mark, Jan, and Jan's sister?"

TOM: "Fine. _____ _____ we need to bring?"
              (11)   (12)

DAVID: "Lots of everything! _____ _____ _____
                            (13)   (14)   (15)
       want?"

TOM: "Hmm. _____ _____ they like to eat?"
             (16)   (17)

DAVID: "Oh, all the usual things. Chicken, potato salad, fruit,

       cookies . . . _____ know, talking about food is making
                     (18)
       me hungry."

TOM: "Me, too! _____ _____ _____ say to going for a
                 (19)   (20)   (21)
       hamburger?"

DAVID: "_____ _____ *you* think? Let's go!"
        (22)   (23)

6

3

want to ⟶ *wanna

PART I

Listen to the tape. You will hear the pairs of sentences listed below. The first sentence in each pair will be spoken with *careful pronunciation*. The second sentence will be spoken with *relaxed pronunciation*.

CAREFUL (SLOW) PRONUNCIATION	RELAXED (FAST) PRONUNCIATION
1. What do you want to do?	1. *Whaddaya *wanna do?
2. I want to eat out.	2. I *wanna eat out.
3. Where do you want to eat?	3. Where do *ya *wanna eat?
4. I want to eat at Tom's Fast Foods.	4. I *wanna eat at Tom's Fast Foods.
5. When do you want to go there?	5. When do *ya *wanna go there?
6. I want to go there now.	6. I *wanna go there now.
7. What do you want to have at Tom's?	7. *Whaddaya *wanna have at Tom's?
8. I want to have a hamburger.	8. I *wanna have a hamburger.
9. What do you want to drink?	9. *Whaddaya *wanna drink?
10. I want to have a coke.	10. I *wanna have a coke.

PART II

Close your book. Listen to the tape. You will hear the 10 sentences with relaxed pronunciation that you heard in Part I. After you hear each sentence, say the same thing, but use *careful pronunciation*.

7

Open your book. Listen to the tape. You will hear a conversation. In it, the speakers will use relaxed pronunciation. As you listen, fill in the blanks with the words you would hear if the speakers were using *careful pronunciation*. Replay the tape as necessary.

AT TOM'S FAST FOODS

DIANE: "_____ _____ _____ _____ _____
(1)   (2)   (3)   (4)   (5)

have?"

CINDY: (looking at the menu) "Let's see. I _____ _____ try
(6)   (7)

the bacon cheeseburger."

DIANE: "That sounds good. _____ _____ _____
(8)   (9)   (10)

_____ _____ drink?"
(11)   (12)

CINDY: "I'm on a diet. I'll have a diet coke."

DIANE: "I _____ _____ try a chocolate malt. I hear the
(13)   (14)

malts here are very good."

DIANE: (to the clerk) "We _____ _____ order two bacon
(15)   (16)

cheeseburgers, a diet coke, and a chocolate malt."

CLERK: "That'll be $3.59."

DIANE: "Here _____ are." (She hands him a five-dollar bill.)
(17)

CLERK: (counting back the change) "3.59, 60, 70, 75, 4.00, and $5.00.

Thank you."

4

```
┌─────────────────────────────────────────────┐
│  going to + verb ─────────→ *gonna          │
└─────────────────────────────────────────────┘
```

NOTE: The ***gonna** pronunciation is used only when *going to* is followed by a verb. In the sentence "I'm going to a movie," for example, the ***gonna** pronunciation is not used because no verb follows *to*. If the sentence is changed to "I'm going to go to a movie," however, the ***gonna** pronunciation is used because the verb *go* follows *to*.

PART I

Listen to the tape. You will hear the pairs of sentences listed below. The first sentence in each pair will be spoken with *careful pronunciation*. The second sentence will be spoken with *relaxed pronunciation*.

CAREFUL (SLOW) PRONUNCIATION	RELAXED (FAST) PRONUNCIATION
1. What are you going to do?	1. *Whaddaya *gonna do?
2. I'm going to a movie.	2. I'm going to a movie.
3. What are you going to see?	3. *Whaddaya *gonna see?
4. I want to see a comedy, but I'm going to see a horror movie.	4. I *wanna see a comedy, but I'm *gonna see a horror movie.
5. Why are you going to see a horror movie?	5. Why are *ya *gonna see a horror movie?
6. Because I'm going to go with my sister and she doesn't want to see a comedy.	6. Because I'm *gonna go with my sister and she doesn't *wanna see a comedy.
7. When are you going to go?	7. When are *ya *gonna go?
8. We're going to go in an hour.	8. We're *gonna go in an hour.
9. What are you going to do after the movie?	9. *Whaddaya *gonna do after the movie?
10. We're probably going to go straight home. We're both going to be pretty sleepy.	10. We're probably *gonna go straight home. We're both *gonna be pretty sleepy.

Close your book. Listen to the tape. You will hear the 10 sentences with relaxed pronunciation that you heard in Part I. After you hear each sentence, say the same thing, but use *careful pronunciation*.

Open your book. Listen to the tape. You will hear a conversation. In it, the speakers will use relaxed pronunciation. As you listen, fill in the blanks with the words you would hear if the speakers were using *careful pronunciation*. Replay the tape as necessary.

THE MONSTER THAT ATE CLEVELAND

RICHARD: "_____ _____ _____
           (1)   (2)   (3)

_____ _____ do tonight?"
    (4)   (5)

JANE: "Nothing. Why?"

RICHARD: "My sister and I are _____ _____ see a movie. Do
              (6)   (7)

_____ _____ _____ come with us?"
  (8)   (9)   (10)

JANE: "Sure. _____ _____ _____
       (11)   (12)   (13)

_____ _____ see?"
  (14)   (15)

RICHARD: *"The Monster That Ate Cleveland."*

JANE: "Wow. I don't _____ _____ miss that. How soon
        (16)   (17)

are _____ _____ _____ leave?"
   (18)   (19)   (20)

RICHARD: "We're _____ _____ leave in about fifteen
     (21)   (22)

minutes. Can _____ be ready to leave then?"
      (23)

JANE: "Sure. See _____ soon."
      (24)

5

| don't know ⟶ *donno |

PART I

Listen to the tape. You will hear the pairs of sentences listed below. The first sentence in each pair will be spoken with *careful pronunciation*. The second sentence will be spoken with *relaxed pronunciation*.

CAREFUL (SLOW) PRONUNCIATION	RELAXED (FAST) PRONUNCIATION
1. I don't know what classes I should take next semester.	1. I *donno what classes I should take next semester.
2. What do you want to take?	2. *Whaddaya *wanna take?
3. Well, I don't know. The problem is that I'm going to be working evenings.	3. Well, I *donno. The problem is that I'm *gonna be working evenings.
4. Are you going to be working all semester?	4. Are *ya *gonna be working all semester?
5. I don't know right now.	5. I *donno right now.
6. What do you want to do when you finish school?	6. *Whaddaya *wanna do when *ya finish school?
7. That's the problem. I don't know.	7. That's the problem. I *donno.
8. Do you want to talk with a counselor?	8. Do *ya *wanna talk with a counselor?
9. I don't know. What do you think?	9. I *donno. *Whaddaya think?
10. I don't know what harm it could do.	10. I *donno what harm it could do.

Close your book. You will hear the 10 sentences with relaxed pronunciation that you heard in Part I. After you hear each sentence, say the same thing, but use *careful pronunciation*.

PART III

Open your book. Listen to the tape. You will hear a conversation. In it, the speakers will use relaxed pronunciation. As you listen, fill in the blanks with the words you would hear if the speakers were using *careful pronunciation*. Replay the tape as necessary.

DECISIONS, DECISIONS

TOM: "I _____ (1) _____ (2) what classes to take.

_____ (3) _____ (4) _____ (5) think I should take?"

VICKIE: "I _____ (6) _____ (7). It depends on what _____ (8)

_____ (9) _____ (10) do after _____ (11) finish school.

_____ (12) _____ (13) _____ (14) _____ (15) _____ (16) do

after _____ (17) graduate?"

TOM: "I _____ (18) _____ (19). I _____ (20) _____ (21) study

engineering at the university, but I _____ (22) _____ (23) if

my grades are good enough."

VICKIE: "I think you should talk to the counselor. I'm _____ (24)

_____ (25) go there now. Do _____ (26)

_____ (27) _____ (28) come with me?"

TOM: "I _____ (29) _____ (30) if it would help.

_____ (31) _____ (32) _____ (33) think?"

VICKIE: "It couldn't hurt. Come on, let's go!"

15

NOTE: *To* is not pronounced ***ta** if it is stressed or if it is not followed by another word. Example: "Who do I give it to?"

PART I

Listen to the tape. You will hear the pairs of sentences listed below. The first sentence in each pair will be spoken with *careful pronunciation*. The second sentence will be spoken with *relaxed pronunciation*.

CAREFUL (SLOW) PRONUNCIATION	RELAXED (FAST) PRONUNCIATION
1. I'm going to Farmer's Market. What bus do I take?	1. I'm going *ta Farmer's Market. What bus do I take?
2. Take Bus 4 to 2nd Street. Then get a transfer.	2. Take Bus 4 *ta 2nd Street. Then get a transfer.
3. Who do I give the transfer to?	3. Who do I give the transfer to?
4. Give it to the bus driver.	4. Give it *ta the bus driver.
5. Then what bus do I change to?	5. Then what bus do I change to?
6. You want to take Bus 89. It goes directly to the market.	6. You *wanna take Bus 89. It goes directly *ta the market.
7. Do I need to have the exact change?	7. Do I need *ta have the exact change?
8. Yes. You need to give the exact change to the bus driver.	8. Yes. *Ya need *ta give the exact change *ta the bus driver.
9. How long will it take to get there?	9. How long will it take *ta get there?
10. Well, you only need to go a few miles, so you'll get to the market in about fifteen minutes.	10. Well, *ya only need *ta go a few miles, so you'll get *ta the market in about fifteen minutes.

PART II

Close your book. Listen to the tape. You will hear the 10 sentences with relaxed pronunciation that you heard in Part I. After you hear each sentence, say the same thing, but use *careful pronunciation*.

17

PART III

Open your book. Listen to the tape. You will hear a conversation. In it, the speakers will use relaxed pronunciation. As you listen, fill in the blanks with the words you would hear if the speakers were using *careful pronunciation*. Replay the tape as necessary.

AT THE BUS STOP

CONNIE: "What bus do I take _____ Farmer's Market?"
                                                    (1)

WOMAN AT THE BUS STOP:

"Take Bus 4 _____ 2nd Street. Then get a transfer
                    (2)

_____ the Market. I'm _____ _____ go shop-
     (3)   (4)   (5)

ping at Farmer's Market, too. I'll tell _____ when
                                              (6)

_____ get off."
     (7)

CONNIE: "Thanks. _____ _____ _____ think is the best
                      (8)   (9)   (10)

place _____ buy souvenirs?"
         (11)

WOMAN: "It depends. _____ _____ _____
                          (12)   (13)   (14)

_____ _____ _____ _____ buy?"
    (15)   (16)   (17)   (18)

CONNIE: "Well, I _____ _____ get some dried fruit
                      (19)   (20)

_____ send my sister and I _____ _____ get
    (21)   (22)   (23)

something unusual _____ send my parents. Right now I
                         (24)

_____ _____ exactly what that's _____
    (25)   (26)   (27)

_____ be."
    (28)

WOMAN: "Well, there are plenty of places _____ shop. I'm sure
                                               (29)

you'll be able _____ find something nice _____
                    (30)   (31)

send your family."

18

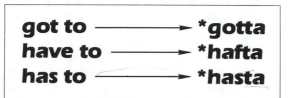

got to	⟶	*gotta
have to	⟶	*hafta
has to	⟶	*hasta

PART I

Listen to the tape. You will hear the pairs of sentences listed below. The first sentence in each pair will be spoken with *careful pronunciation*. The second sentence will be spoken with *relaxed pronunciation*.

CAREFUL (SLOW) PRONUNCIATION

1. My tooth's going to drive me crazy. It has to come out.
2. Then you've got to make an appointment with a dentist.
3. I've got to find one first. I don't know any dentists.
4. I have to go downtown. Come on. I'll take you to *my* dentist.
5. I can't. I have to study.
6. After you study, are you going to go to the dentist?
7. No. Then I've got to get some gas.
8. *Then* are you going to go to the dentist?
9. Well, no. After that, I have to go to the bank.
10. After you go to the bank, you've *got to* go to the dentist. Your tooth *has to* be taken care of!

RELAXED (FAST) PRONUNCIATION

1. My tooth's *gonna drive me crazy. It *hasta come out.
2. Then you've *gotta make an appointment with a dentist.
3. I've *gotta find one first. I *donno any dentists.
4. I *hafta go downtown. Come on. I'll take *ya *ta *my* dentist.
5. I can't. I *hafta study.
6. After *ya study, are *ya *gonna go *ta the dentist?
7. No. Then I've *gotta get some gas.
8. *Then* are *ya *gonna go *ta the dentist?
9. Well, no. After that, I *hafta go *ta the bank.
10. After *ya go *ta the bank, you've *gotta go *ta the dentist. Your tooth *hasta be taken care of!

PART II

Close your book. Listen to the tape. You will hear the 10 sentences with relaxed pronunciation that you heard in Part I. After you hear each sentence, say the same thing, but use *careful pronunciation.*

PART III

Open your book. Listen to the tape. You will hear a conversation. In it, the speakers will use relaxed pronunciation. As you listen, fill in the blanks with the words you would hear if the speakers were using *careful pronunciation.* Replay the tape as necessary.

TO PULL OR NOT TO PULL

JOE: "The dentist has _____ _____ see me soon. He
(1)   (2)

_____ _____ do something about my tooth.
(3)   (4)

It really hurts!"

TERRY: "Don't worry. I'm sure the dentist is _____ _____ be
(5)   (6)

able _____ help _____. _____ won't _____
(7)   (8)   (9)   (10)

_____ wait very long."
(11)

JOE: "_____ don't think he's _____ _____ tell me he
(12)   (13)   (14)

_____ _____ pull my tooth, do _____?"
(15)   (16)   (17)

TERRY: "I _____ _____. If he _____ _____ pull it, he
(18)   (19)   (20)   (21)

will, but I'm sure he'll try _____ save it if he can."
(22)

JOE: "Well, I guess I won't _____ _____ wait any longer
(23)   (24)

_____ find out. He's ready _____ see me now."
(25)   (26)

(Later)

TERRY: "What happened? You've _____ _____ tell me!"
(27)   (28)

JOE: "Well, first he said he'd _____ _____ check the tooth."
(29)   (30)

TERRY: "Then what happened? Did he _____ _____ pull it?"
(31)   (32)

JOE: "No. He decided _____ fill it, not pull it. But he said I've
(33)

_____ _____ come back tomorrow. He's _____
(34)   (35)   (36)

_____ take some x-rays and he _____ _____
(37)   (38)   (39)

check my other teeth."

21

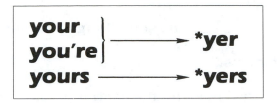

NOTE: *Your* and *you're* are not pronounced ***yer** if stressed.

PART I

Listen to the tape. You will hear the pairs of sentences listed below. The first sentence in each pair will be spoken with *careful pronunciation*. The second sentence will be spoken with *relaxed pronunciation*.

CAREFUL (SLOW) PRONUNCIATION	RELAXED (FAST) PRONUNCIATION
1. How's your mother?	1. How's *yer mother?
2. She's fine. How's yours?	2. She's fine. How's *yers?
3. She's fine, too. I hear your brother's going to start college.	3. She's fine, too. I hear *yer brother's *gonna start college.
4. That's right. And how about *your* brother? How's *he*?	4. That's right. And how about *your* brother? How's *he*?
5. He's fine. He's with your sister tonight.	5. He's fine. He's with *yer sister tonight.
6. You know, I think your brother and my sister want to get married.	6. *Ya know, I think *yer brother and my sister *wanna get married.
7. I think maybe you're right.	7. I think maybe *yer right.
8. I think you're going to have to tell your parents about them.	8. I think *yer *gonna *hafta tell *yer parents about them.
9. No, I think we should wait for your sister and my brother to say something.	9. No, I think we should wait for *yer sister and my brother *ta say something.
10. I don't know. It's hard to know what to do.	10. I *donno. It's hard *ta know what *ta do.

Close your book. Listen to the tape. You will hear the 10 sentences with relaxed pronunciation that you heard in Part I. After you hear each sentence, say the same thing, but use *careful pronunciation.*

PART III

Open your book. Listen to the tape. You will hear a conversation. In it, the speakers will use relaxed pronunciation. As you listen, fill in the blanks with the words you would hear if the speakers were using *careful pronunciation.* Replay the tape as necessary.

WEDDING BELLS

CINDY: "How's _____ brother?"
        (1)

TINA: "He's all right, I guess. How's _____ sister?"
        (2)

CINDY: "Oh, she's fine. Say, somebody told me _____ sister's
        (3)

        _____ _____ get married _____ my brother.
        (4)   (5)   (6)

        Do _____ know anything about it?"
           (7)

TINA: "No, I _____ _____ a thing about it. Do _____
              (8)   (9)   (10)

        think _____ family knows?"
              (11)

CINDY: "No, I don't think so. Do _____ think _____ knows?"
                                  (12)   (13)

TINA: "I'm sure they don't. _____ _____ _____ think
                              (14)   (15)   (16)

        we should do? Should we tell our families?"

CINDY: "No, I don't think so. I think _____ brother and my
                                        (17)

        sister _____ _____ tell them."
               (18)   (19)

TINA: "_____ right, I guess. So we know what *they've*
         (20)

        _____ _____ do. But _____ _____ *we*
        (21)   (22)   (23)   (24)

        _____ _____ do?"
        (25)   (26)

CINDY: "I've _____ _____ make sure my sister tells *my*
              (27)   (28)

        family, and you've _____ _____ make sure
                           (29)   (30)

        _____ brother tells _____."
        (31)   (32)

TINA: "_____ idea sounds like a good one. I guess that's what
         (33)

        we're _____ _____ _____ _____ do."
              (34)   (35)   (36)   (37)

24

```
/t/ + you  ──────────▶ *cha

/t/ + your  ⎫
           ⎬ ──────▶ *cher
/t/ + you're ⎭
```

PART I

Listen to the tape. You will hear the pairs of sentences listed below. The first sentence in each pair will be spoken with *careful pronunciation*. The second sentence will be spoken with *relaxed pronunciation*.

CAREFUL (SLOW) PRONUNCIATION	RELAXED (FAST) PRONUNCIATION
1. Can't you find an apartment?	1. Can't *cha find an apartment?
2. No, I can't. The rent you have to pay is just too much.	2. No, I can't. The rent *cha *hafta pay is just too much.
3. You know, my brother might be able to get you an apartment.	3. *Ya know, my brother might be able *ta get *cha an apartment.
4. Well, I don't want your brother to spend too much time on it.	4. Well, I don't want *cher brother *ta spend too much time on it.
5. No problem. He knows that you're new in town.	5. No problem. He knows that *cher new in town.
6. I want you to thank him in advance.	6. I want *cha *ta thank him in advance.
7. Of course. Tell me what you're looking for.	7. Of course. Tell me what *cher looking for.
8. I don't know, really. Don't you think a one-bedroom furnished apartment would be nice?	8. I *donno, really. Don't *cha think a one-bedroom furnished apartment would be nice?

25

9. Yes, but I think that you won't be able to find a cheap one near here.

10. Well, I've always said, "Don't you ever give up."

9. Yes, but I think that *cha won't be able *ta find a cheap one near here.

10. Well, I've always said, "Don't *cha ever give up."

PART II

Close your book. Listen to the tape. You will hear the 10 sentences with relaxed pronunciation that you heard in Part I. After you hear each sentence, say the same thing, but use *careful pronunciation*.

PART III

Open your book. Listen to the tape. You will hear a conversation. In it, the speakers will use relaxed pronunciation. As you listen, fill in the blanks with the words you would hear if the speakers were using *careful pronunciation*. Replay the tape as necessary.

LOOKING FOR AN APARTMENT

SAM: "I _____ _____ _____ help me find an
                 (1)   (2)   (3)

apartment."

MARK: "Sure. Do _____ know _____ _____
                      (4)   (5)   (6)

looking for?"

SAM: "The important thing is that it's _____ _____
                                          (7)   (8)

be cheap."

MARK: "Then why _____ _____ try _____ find a
                      (9)   (10)   (11)

roommate? That'd make it cheaper for both of _____ ."
                                                          (12)

SAM: "_____ _____ saying's true, but right now I don't
        (13)   (14)

_____ _____ have a roommate."
    (15)   (16)

MARK: "O.K. That reminds me. _____ _____ sister's place
                                 (17)   (18)

there's a pool. _____ _____ _____
                (19)   (20)   (21)

_____ _____ find a place that has one, too,
    (22)   (23)

_____ _____?"
    (24)   (25)

SAM: "I _____ _____ . I _____ _____ find a
      (26)   (27)   (28)   (29)

cheap apartment!"

MARK: "Okay, okay. _____ _____ worry. We'll find just
                    (30)   (31)

_____ _____ looking for sooner or later."
(32)   (33)

28

10

"ing" endings ──────→ *-in'

NOTE: Most native English speakers do not use the ***-in'** pronunciation for all "—ing" endings. The ***-in'** pronunciation is most often used with progressive tenses of verbs.

PART I

Listen to the tape. You will hear the pairs of sentences listed below. The first sentence in each pair will be spoken with *careful pronunciation*. The second sentence will be spoken with *relaxed pronunciation*.

CAREFUL (SLOW) PRONUNCIATION	RELAXED (FAST) PRONUNCIATION
1. What are you doing?	1. *Whaddaya *doin'?
2. I'm trying on a new suit.	2. I'm *tryin' on a new suit.
3. I'm going to be joining you in a minute.	3. I'm *gonna be *joinin' *ya in a minute.
4. Oh. What are you going to be trying on?	4. Oh. *Whaddaya *gonna be *tryin' on?
5. I'm going to be trying on some suits, too.	5. I'm *gonna be *tryin' on some suits, too.
6. Will you be buying many new clothes?	6. Will *ya be *buyin' many new clothes?
7. No. I'm only thinking about getting a new suit.	7. No. I'm only *thinkin' about *gettin' a new suit.
8. That's nice. Are you going to be buying it today?	8. That's nice. Are *ya *gonna be *buyin' it today?
9. No. Today I'm just looking around.	9. No. Today I'm just *lookin' around.
10. Well, I hope you find what you're looking for.	10. Well, I hope *ya find what *cher *lookin' for.

PART II

Close your book. Listen to the tape. You will hear the 10 sentences with relaxed pronunciation that you heard in Part I. After you hear each sentence, say the same thing, but use *careful pronunciation*

PART III

Listen to the tape. You will hear a conversation. In it, the speakers will use relaxed pronunciation. As you listen, fill in the blanks with the words you would hear if the speakers were using *careful pronunciation*. Replay the tape as necessary.

SHOPPING

CLERK: "Can I help _____?"
        (1)

JOHN: "Yes. I'm _____ for some jeans."
       (2)

CLERK: "Do _____ _____ _____ see straight legs or
           (3)   (4)   (5)

flared legs?"

JOHN: "I'm _____ for straight legs."
            (6)

CLERK: "Here _____ are. Try them on in the dressing room over
              (7)

there."

JOHN: "Thank you."

(A Few Minutes Later)

JOHN: "I'm _____ _____ _____ _____ have a
            (8)   (9)   (10)   (11)

larger size. I'm _____ trouble _____ in these."
                   (12)   (13)

CLERK: "I'm sorry, but we don't have any larger sizes in that style.

Why _____ _____ try _____ around for some-
      (14)   (15)   (16)

thing else?"

JOHN: "Thanks. I'll do that. Do _____ have any suggestions?"
                                 (17)

CLERK: "Well, _____ might be interested in _____ a look at
              (18)   (19)

our designer jeans. A lot of people have been _____
                                               (20)

designer jeans lately."

JOHN: "That sounds good. Where are they?"

CLERK: "Behind _____. _____ _____ right in front
                (21)   (22)   (23)

of them."

31

11

What are you |
What you | ⟶ ***Whacha**

NOTE: ***Whacha** is even more informal than ***whaddaya**. First, it is a very informal way of saying *what are you*. It is also one of the most common examples of /t/ + *you* (see Lesson 9). And finally, ***whacha** is occasionally used for *what do you*.

PART I

Listen to the tape. You will hear the pairs of sentences listed below. The first sentence in each pair will be spoken with *careful pronunciation*. The second sentence will be spoken with *relaxed pronunciation*.

CAREFUL (SLOW) PRONUNCIATION	RELAXED (FAST) PRONUNCIATION
1. What are you doing back there?	1. *Whacha *doin' back there?
2. I'm doing what you told me to do. I'm trimming your hair.	2. I'm *doin' *whacha told me *ta do. I'm *trimmin' *yer hair.
3. How much are you taking off in the back?	3. How much are *ya *takin' off in the back?
4. I'm taking off what you told me—about an inch.	4. I'm *takin' off *whacha told me—about an inch.
5. What are you going to do to the front?	5. *Whacha *gonna do *ta the front?
6. Oh, I've got to even it out a little.	6. Oh, I've *gotta even it out a little.
7. What do you plan to do when you finish?	7. *Whacha plan *ta do when *ya finish?
8. I don't know what you mean. Do you mean when I finish your hair?	8. I *donno *whacha mean. Do *ya mean when I finish *yer hair?

32

9. Yes. What are you going to
   do after you finish it?

9. Yes. *Whacha *gonna do
   after *ya finish it?

10. Oh, I'm going to go to Barber
    School. You're my first
    haircut!

10. Oh, I'm *gonna go *ta Barber
    School. *Yer my first
    haircut!

PART II

Close your book. Listen to the tape. You will hear the 10 sentences with relaxed pronunciation that you heard in Part I. After you hear each sentence, say the same thing, but use *careful pronunciation*.

PART III

Open your book. Listen to the tape. You will hear a conversation. In it, the speakers will use relaxed pronunciation. As you listen, fill in the blanks with the words you would hear if the speakers were using *careful pronunciation*. Replay the tape as necessary.

GOING TO THE BARBER

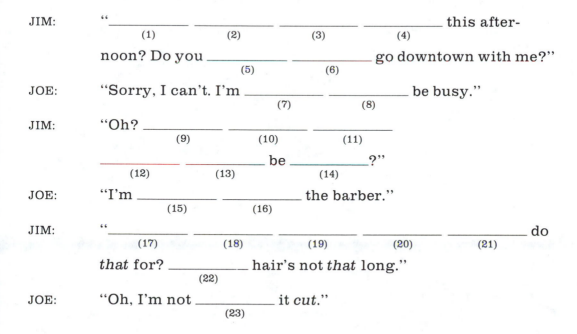

JIM: "_____ _____ _____ _____ this after-
             (1)   (2)   (3)   (4)

noon? Do you _____ _____ go downtown with me?"
                  (5)   (6)

JOE: "Sorry, I can't. I'm _____ _____ be busy."
                                  (7)   (8)

JIM: "Oh? _____ _____ _____
               (9)   (10)   (11)

_____ _____ be _____?"
    (12)   (13)   (14)

JOE: "I'm _____ _____ the barber."
               (15)   (16)

JIM: "_____ _____ _____ _____ _____ do
              (17)   (18)   (19)   (20)   (21)

that for? _____ hair's not *that* long."
                (22)

JOE: "Oh, I'm not _____ it *cut*."
                          (23)

33

JIM: "I don't understand _____ _____ mean.
               (24)   (25)

_____ _____ _____ _____ _____ the
  (26)   (27)   (28)   (29)   (30)

barber for if _____ not _____ _____ hair cut?"
               (31)   (32)   (33)

JOE: "Oh, I'm just _____ it trimmed. Say, tell me _____
                  (34)   (35)

_____ think about my sideburns. Are they too long?"
  (36)

JIM: "Maybe. It'll depend on how _____ hair looks when it's
                           (37)

trimmed. Why _____ _____ just tell the barber
             (38)   (39)

_____ _____ _____ _____ hair _____
  (40)   (41)   (42)   (43)   (44)

look like? Let *him* worry about _____ the sideburns
                          (45)

right."

JOE: "_____ _____ say makes sense. I guess that's what
     (46)   (47)

I'll do."

12

```
/d/ + you ──────► *ja
/d/ + your ──────► *jer
```

PART I

Listen to the tape. You will hear the pairs of sentences listed below. The first sentence in each pair will be spoken with *careful pronunciation*. The second sentence will be spoken with *relaxed pronunciation*.

CAREFUL (SLOW) PRONUNCIATION	RELAXED (FAST) PRONUNCIATION
1. Could you put in $5.00 worth of regular?	1. Could *ja put in $5.00 worth of regular?
2. All right. Would you like me to check under the hood?	2. All right. Would *ja like me *ta check under the hood?
3. Yes, please. And could you also check the tires?	3. Yes, please. And could *ja also check the tires?
4. Sure. How many pounds should your tires have?	4. Sure. How many pounds should *jer tires have?
5. Oh, I don't know. I told you the last time, but I forgot.	5. Oh, I *donno. I told *ja the last time, but I forgot.
6. That's all right. By the way, I found your problem under the hood.	6. That's all right. By the way, I found *jer problem under the hood.
7. Did you say I have a problem under the hood?	7. Did *ja say I have a problem under the hood?
8. Yes. When's the last time you had your oil checked? You're leaking oil.	8. Yes. When's the last time *ya had *jer oil checked? *Yer *leakin' oil.
9. Did you say I'm leaking oil?	9. Did *ja say I'm *leakin' oil?
10. Yes. Did you know that you're two quarts low?	10. Yes. Did *ja know that *cher two quarts low?

PART II

Close your book. Listen to the tape. You will hear the 10 sentences with relaxed pronunciation that you heard in Part I. After you hear each sentence, say the same thing, but use *careful pronunciation*.

PART III

Open your book. Listen to the tape. You will hear a conversation. In it, the speakers will use relaxed pronunciation. As you listen, fill in the blanks with the words you would hear if the speakers were using *careful pronunciation*. Replay the tape as necessary.

FILL IT UP

ATTENDANT:

      "Would _____ like me _____ put in unleaded?"
               (1)   (2)

AL:

      "Yes, unleaded. And could _____ check under the hood?
                                 (3)

      I'm _____ _____ be _____ a long way, so I
              (4)   (5)   (6)

      _____ _____ be sure everything's all right."
         (7)   (8)

(A Few Minutes Later)

ATTENDANT:

"When's the last time _____ had _____ oil
(9)   (10)

checked? _____ a quart low on oil and _____ really
(11)   (12)

need _____ oil filter replaced. _____ want me
(13)   (14)

_____ add the oil and put in a new filter, don't
(15)

_____?"
(16)

AL:

"Well, I _____ _____. I guess so. But I don't have
(17)   (18)

much money, so would _____ do it as cheaply as
(19)

_____ can?"
(20)

ATTENDANT:

"Okay."

(A Few Minutes Later)

ATTENDANT:

"That's _____ _____ be $23.50 for the gas, oil, and
(21)   (22)

filter."

AL:

"_____ take credit cards, don't _____? Or would
(23)   (24)

_____ take a check?"
(25)

ATTENDANT:

"Only our own credit cards. No checks."

AL:

"Oh. Then I'm _____ _____ have a slight problem!"
(26)   (27)

13

NOTE: *Or* is not pronounced ***er** when stressed.

PART I

Listen to the tape. You will hear the pairs of sentences listed below. The first sentence in each pair will be spoken with *careful pronunciation*. The second sentence will be spoken with *relaxed pronunciation*.

CAREFUL (SLOW) PRONUNCIATION	RELAXED (FAST) PRONUNCIATION
1. Would you like coffee or tea?	1. Would *ja like coffee *er tea?
2. Tea, please. Do you have lemon?	2. Tea, please. Do *ya have lemon?
3. Sure. Do you want to order now or do you want to wait?	3. Sure. Do *ya *wanna order now *er do *ya *wanna wait?
4. I want to order now. Which would you recommend—the chicken or the fish?	4. I *wanna order now. Which would *ja recommend—the chicken *er the fish?
5. Either the chicken *or* the fish is good.	5. Either the chicken *or* the fish is good.
6. Do I have a choice of soup or salad?	6. Do I have a choice of soup *er salad?
7. Yes. The soups are chicken noodle or beef noodle.	7. Yes. The soups are chicken noodle *er beef noodle.
8. I don't want to have chicken noodle *or* beef noodle. What dressing do you put on the salad?	8. I don't *wanna have chicken noodle *or* beef noodle. What dressing do *ya put on the salad?
9. We have bleu cheese or thousand island.	9. We have bleu cheese *er thousand island.
10. Then I'm going to have the chicken dinner and salad with bleu cheese dressing. I'll have cake or pie for dessert. I'm going to decide about dessert later.	10. Then I'm *gonna have the chicken dinner and salad with bleu cheese dressing. I'll have cake *er pie for dessert. I'm *gonna decide about dessert later.

39

PART II

Close your book. Listen to the tape. You will hear the 10 sentences with relaxed pronunciation that you heard in Part I. After you hear each sentence, say the same thing, but use *careful pronunciation*.

PART III

Open your book. Listen to the tape. You will hear a conversation. In it, the speakers will use relaxed pronunciation. As you listen, fill in the blanks with the words you would hear if the speakers were using *careful pronunciation*. Replay the tape as necessary.

AT THE COFFEE SHOP

RICHARD: "_____ _____ like _____ eat here, _____
             (1)   (2)   (3)   (4)

do _____ _____ _____ try Tom's Fast Foods?"
       (5)   (6)   (7)

SUSAN: "We'd better eat here. We've _____ _____ get back
                                (8)   (9)

_____ work in an hour."
   (10)

RICHARD: "Do _____ _____ _____ have a cocktail
           (11)   (12)   (13)

_____ some coffee _____ something else
  (14)   (15)

_____ start?"
  (16)

SUSAN: "Oh, I _____ _____ . Coffee, I guess."
           (17)   (18)

RICHARD: "Here's our waitress."

WAITRESS: "Are _____ ready _____ order?"
         (19)   (20)

RICHARD: "Yes. I'm _____ _____ have a turkey sandwich
         (21)   (22)

with cheese. Do _____ have cheddar cheese, _____
          (23)   (24)

just American.?"

WAITRESS: "We have both."

RICHARD: "Then I'd like cheddar, and some coffee _____ drink."
                                (25)

(to Susan) "_____ _____ _____
            (26)   (27)   (28)

_____ _____ have, Susan?"
  (29)   (30)

SUSAN: "Oh, I'll have a tuna sandwich. Do _____ have rye
                              (31)

bread, _____ just white?"
     (32)

WAITRESS: "We have both. _____ _____ like rye?"
                 (33)   (34)

SUSAN: "Yes, please, and some coffee."

14

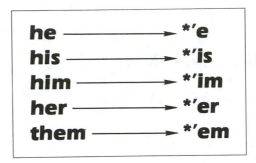

he	⟶	*'e
his	⟶	*'is
him	⟶	*'im
her	⟶	*'er
them	⟶	*'em

NOTE: These pronunciations are not used when *he*, *his*, *him*, *her*, and *them* are stressed.

PART I

Listen to the tape. You will hear the pairs of sentences listed below. The first sentence in each pair will be spoken with *careful pronunciation*. The second sentence will be spoken with *relaxed pronunciation*.

CAREFUL (SLOW) PRONUNCIATION	RELAXED (FAST) PRONUNCIATION
1. Tell him what you want.	1. Tell *'im what *cha want.
2. I want to mail these two packages to my parents. I want them to get them as soon as possible.	2. I *wanna mail these two packages *ta my parents. I want *'em *ta get *'em as soon as possible.
3. How fast do you want them to get them?	3. How fast do *ya want *'em to get *'em?
4. Faster than my brother got the package I sent *him*. I sent him the package last month, and do you know when he got it?—Last week!	4. Faster than my brother got the package I sent *him*. I sent *'im the package last month, and do *ya know when *'e got it?—Last week!
5. How did you send it to him?	5. How did *ja send it to *'im?
6. I sent his package by regular mail.	6. I sent *'is package by regular mail.
7. But I sent my sister a package, and it only took her four days to get it. I sent *her* package by airmail.	7. But I sent my sister a package, and it only took *'er four days *ta get it. I sent *her* package by airmail.

8. So do you want to send them by airmail or regular mail?

9. When will my parents get them if I send them by airmail?

10. They'll get them within a week.

8. So do *ya *wanna send *'em by airmail *er regular mail?

9. When will my parents get *'em if I send *'em by airmail?

10. They'll get *'em within a week.

PART II

Close your book. Listen to the tape. You will hear the 10 sentences with relaxed pronunciation that you heard in Part I. After you hear each sentence, say the same thing, but use *careful pronunciation.*

PART III

Open your book. Listen to the tape. You will hear a conversation. In it, the speakers will use relaxed pronunciation. As you listen, fill in the blanks with the words you would hear if the speakers were using *careful pronunciation.* Replay the tape as necessary.

AT THE POST OFFICE

DAVID: "I _____ _____ send these packages _____
            (1)   (2)   (3)

New York."

CLERK: "How do _____ _____ _____ send _____ ?"
                    (4)   (5)   (6)   (7)

DAVID: "Well, I'm _____ _____ _____ my uncle, and I
                   (8)   (9)   (10)

_____ _____ get _____ to _____ by Fri-
  (11)   (12)   (13)   (14)

day. _____ _____ _____ suggest?"
     (15)   (16)   (17)

CLERK: "I _____ _____ , but I'll go talk _____ my super-
        (18)   (19)   (20)

visor. I'll ask _____ what the fastest way would be."
          (21)

DAVID: "Tell _____ that they _____ _____ get
        (22)   (23)   (24)

_____ my uncle as soon as possible, and that _____
  (25)   (26)

_____ _____ get _____ no later than Friday."
  (27)   (28)   (29)

CLERK: "I'll tell _____ ."
          (30)

(A Few Minutes Later)

DAVID: "What was _____ advice?"
          (31)

44

CLERK: "She says you should send _____ to _____ by
                               (32)   (33)

Express Mail _____ Air Mail Special Delivery. Express
                          (34)

Mail's the fastest, but it's expensive. If you send _____
                                       (35)

_____ _____ uncle by Air Mail Special Delivery,
(36)   (37)

it's cheaper, but _____ might not get _____ for
                  (38)   (39)

several days."

DAVID: "If I send _____ packages to _____ by Air Mail
             (40)   (41)

Special Delivery, will _____ get _____ by Friday?"
                  (42)   (43)

CLERK: "Maybe. If _____ luck's good, _____ will, but I
         (44)   (45)

can't promise anything."

DAVID: "Well, I guess I'll send my uncle _____ packages by
                             (46)

Express Mail, then."

15

PART I

Listen to the tape. You will hear the pairs of sentences listed below. The first sentence in each pair will be spoken with *careful pronunciation*. The second sentence will be spoken with *relaxed pronunciation*.

CAREFUL (SLOW) PRONUNCIATION	RELAXED (FAST) PRONUNCIATION
1. I want to get a taxi to take me to the Galaxy Hotel on 3rd and Grand.	1. I *wanna get a taxi *ta take me *ta the Galaxy Hotel on 3rd *'n' Grand.
2. Take your bags over there and wait.	2. Take *yer bags over there *'n' wait.
3. Taxi! Taxi! I want to go to the Galaxy Hotel on 3rd and Grand.	3. Taxi! Taxi! I *wanna go *ta the Galaxy Hotel on 3rd *'n' Grand.
4. Did you say 3rd and Grand?	4. Did *ja say 3rd *'n' Grand?
5. That's right. 3rd and Grand.	5. That's right. 3rd *'n' Grand.
6. Sorry. That hotel's being rebuilt. They've got to repair the fire and water damages.	6. Sorry. That hotel's *bein' rebuilt. They've *gotta repair the fire *'n' water damages.
7. What about the Wyatt Hotel on 10th and Garden?	7. What about the Wyatt Hotel on 10th *'n' Garden?
8. 10th and Garden?	8. 10th *'n' Garden?
9. That's right. 10th and Garden. The Wyatt Hotel. Here are my bags.	9. That's right. 10th *'n' Garden. The Wyatt Hotel. Here are my bags.
10. Fine. I'll put them in the trunk and then we'll go to the Wyatt.	10. Fine. I'll put *'em in the trunk *'n' then we'll go *ta the Wyatt.

PART II

Close your book. Listen to the tape. You will hear the 10 sentences with relaxed pronunciation that you heard in Part I. After you hear each sentence, say the same thing, but use *careful pronunciation*.

PART III

Open your book. Listen to the tape. You will hear a conversation. In it, the speakers will use relaxed pronunciation. As you listen, fill in the blanks with the words you would hear if the speakers were using *careful pronunciation*. Replay the tape as necessary.

TAXI, TAXI

RON: "Let's get a taxi _____ then I _____ _____
         (1)   (2)   (3)

have lunch. I'm _____!"
                   (4)

TIM: "Sure. Taxi! Taxi!" (to the taxi driver) "We're _____
                                                        (5)

_____ stay at the Garden Hotel on Garden Avenue
   (6)

_____ 5th Street."
   (7)

TAXI DRIVER:
         "Sure. Are those _____ bags over there?"
                              (8)

RON: "Yes."

DRIVER: "I'll put _____ in the trunk _____ then we'll get
                     (9)   (10)

_____ later."
   (11)

(Half an Hour Later)

TIM: (whispers to Ron) "_____ _____ _____ think
                           (12)   (13)   (14)

we should tip _____?"
                 (15)

RON: (whispers to Tim) "Oh, I _____ _____ . About a
                                 (16)   (17)

dollar _____ a half, I guess."
          (18)

DRIVER: "Here we are. Now let me go _____
                                       (19)

_____ _____ bags."
   (20)   (21)

TIM: (to the driver) "Here's _____ money _____ thank
                                (22)   (23)

you very much."

DRIVER: "Thank *you*."

PART I

Listen to the tape. You will hear the pairs of sentences listed below. The first sentence in each pair will be spoken with *careful pronunciation*. The second sentence will be spoken with *relaxed pronunciation*.

CAREFUL (SLOW) PRONUNCIATION

1. Can you see?
2. Yes, I can see.
3. Can you pass the popcorn?
4. Sure. Can you move down a little?
5. All right. Can you see them yet?
6. I can see them but I can't hear them. Can *you*?
7. Yes. I can hear them.
8. Now *I* can hear them, too.
9. They're coming on the stage. Can you see them?
10. Yes, I can see them. Wow! This is really going to be a good concert!

RELAXED (FAST) PRONUNCIATION

1. *Kin *ya see?
2. Yes, I *kin see.
3. *Kin *ya pass the popcorn?
4. Sure. *Kin *ya move down a little?
5. All right. *Kin *ya see *'em yet?
6. I *kin see *'em but I can't hear *'em. *Kin *you*?
7. Yes. I *kin hear *'em.
8. Now *I* *kin hear *'em, too.
9. They're *comin' on the stage. *Kin *ya see *'em?
10. Yes, I *kin see *'em. Wow! This is really *gonna be a good concert!

PART II

Close your book. Listen to the tape. You will hear the 10 sentences with relaxed pronunciation that you heard in Part I. After you hear each sentence, say the same thing, but use *careful pronunciation*.

PART III

Open your book. Listen to the tape. You will hear a conversation. In it, the speakers will use relaxed pronunciation. As you listen, fill in the blanks with the words you would hear if the speakers were using *careful pronunciation*. Replay the tape as necessary.

THE ROCK CONCERT

JERRY: "_____ _____ see the stage?"
             (1)   (2)

TINA: "What _____ _____ say?"
               (3)   (4)

JERRY: (louder) "I said, '_____ _____ see the stage?'"
                      (5)   (6)

TINA: "Sure, I _____ see it. _____ _____ love rock
               (7)   (8)   (9)

concerts?"

JERRY: "What's that? _____ _____ speak a little louder?"
                  (10)   (11)

TINA: (loudly) "I said, '_____ _____ love rock concerts?'"
                   (12)   (13)

JERRY: "Oh. Sure, I like _____ a lot. Look! _____
                    (14)   (15)

_____ see the band? They're about _____ come
(16)   (17)

on stage!"

(Wild Applause)

TINA: "What? _____ _____ speak up? I can't hear
            (18)   (19)

_____ !"
(20)

JERRY: (very loudly) "I said, 'Look! The band's _____ on
                          (21)

the stage!'"

TINA: "You'll _____ _____ speak louder, Jerry. The
           (22)   (23)

band's about _____ come on stage, and I _____
           (24)   (25)

barely hear _____ !"
           (26)

17

PART I

Listen to the tape. You will hear the pairs of sentences listed below. The first sentence in each pair will be spoken with *careful pronunciation*. The second sentence will be spoken with *relaxed pronunciation*.

CAREFUL (SLOW) PRONUNCIATION	RELAXED (FAST) PRONUNCIATION
1. I've invited a lot of people to the party tonight.	1. I've invited a lot *a people *ta the party tonight.
2. Then we'll have to go shopping. It's a quarter of three now.	2. Then we'll *hafta go shopping. It's a quarter *a three now.
3. Shouldn't we get a carton of cokes?	3. Shouldn't we get a carton *a cokes?
4. Yes. I also want to get a bag of pretzels.	4. Yes. I also *wanna get a bag *a pretzels.
5. And we'll also need a couple of boxes of cookies.	5. *'N' we'll also need a couple *a boxes *a cookies.
6. And a few bags of potato chips.	6. *'N' a few bags *a potato chips.
7. Are you going to get a couple of bottles of orange juice?	7. Are *ya *gonna get a couple *a bottles *a orange juice?
8. Yes. And a couple of other things, too.	8. Yes. *'N' a couple *a other things, too.
9. Am I going to have time to cash a check? It's ten of three now.	9. Am I *gonna have time *ta cash a check? It's ten *a three now.
10. Don't cash a check. I've got plenty of money.	10. Don't cash a check. I've got plenty *a money.

Close your book. Listen to the tape. You will hear the 10 sentences with relaxed pronunciation that you heard in Part I. After you hear each sentence, say the same thing, but use *careful pronunciation*.

Open your book. Listen to the tape. You will hear a conversation. In it, the speakers will use relaxed pronunciation. As you listen, fill in the blanks with the words you would hear if the speakers were using *careful pronunciation*. Replay the tape as necessary.

AT THE SUPERMARKET

JULIE: "Where's the milk?"

CHECKER: "It's down aisle 25 in the corner _____ the store."
                                 (1)

JULIE: "Thanks." (to herself) "I'll get three cartons _____ milk
                                                 (2)

_____ a few bottles _____ orange juice." (to
(3)   (4)

another employee) "Excuse me. _____ _____ tell
                                 (5)   (6)

me where the bags _____ potato chips are?"
                         (7)

CLERK: "Sure. Go down aisle 10. They're at the end _____ the
                                    (8)

aisle. They're next _____ the packages _____ nuts."
                   (9)   (10)

JULIE: "Thank you." (to another shopper) "_____ _____
                             (11)   (12)

tell me what time it is?"

SHOPPER: "Sure. It's ten _____ four."
                    (13)

JULIE: "Thank you." (to herself) "I've _____ _____ get
                               (14)   (15)

_____ _____ I'm _____ _____ be late! I
(16)   (17)   (18)   (19)

have a group _____ people _____ _____ my
              (20)   (21)   (22)

house in two hours!"

should could would must may might	+ have + past participle →	*shoulda *coulda *woulda *musta *maya *mighta

NOTE: Modals + *have* + past participles are also commonly contracted. When contracted, they sound like *should of, *could of, *would of, etc. The pronunciations ***shoulda**, ***coulda**, etc. are more informal than the contracted forms. This pronunciation is used even when the modal is negative.

PART I

Listen to the tape. You will hear the pairs of sentences listed below. The first sentence in each pair will be spoken with *careful pronunciation*. The second sentence will be spoken with *relaxed pronunciation*.

CAREFUL (SLOW) PRONUNCIATION

1. Oh no! We should have been at Judy's house at a quarter of seven!
2. Well, you could have gotten directions ahead of time. That would have helped.
3. Yes, you're right. I must have been crazy to try to find her house out here.
4. Wait a minute. I think there may have been a gas station back there.

RELAXED (FAST) PRONUNCIATION

1. Oh no! We *shoulda been at Judy's house at a quarter *a seven!
2. Well, *ya *coulda gotten directions ahead *a time. That *woulda helped.
3. Yes, *yer right. I *musta been crazy *ta try *ta find *'er house out here.
4. Wait a minute. I think there *maya been a gas station back there.

5. Where did you see it?
6. It might have been back a mile or so.
7. I don't know. I think I would have seen it.
8. You might have missed seeing it while we were talking.
9. You're probably right. If I'd seen it, we could have stopped there and asked directions to Judy's house.
10. Would have, might have, could have—Why don't we go back and get directions?

5. Where did *ja see it?
6. It *mighta been back a mile *er so.
7. I *donno. I think I *woulda seen it.
8. *Ya *mighta missed *seein' it while we were *talkin'.
9. *Yer probably right. If I'd seen it, we *coulda stopped there *'n' asked directions *ta Judy's house.
10. *Woulda, *mighta, *coulda— Why don't we go back *'n' get directions?

PART II

Close your book. Listen to the tape. You will hear the 10 sentences with relaxed pronunciation that you heard in Part I. After you hear each sentence, say the same thing, but use *careful pronunciation*.

PART III

Open your book. Listen to the tape. You will hear a conversation. In it, the speakers will use relaxed pronunciation. As you listen, fill in the blanks with the words you would hear if the speakers were using *careful pronunciation*. Replay the tape as necessary.

GETTING DIRECTIONS

DON: (to Sandy) "We're lost. _____ _____ _____
(1)   (2)   (3)

think we should do?"

SANDY: "Well, maybe we _____ _____ taken a left on Clark
(4)   (5)

Street."

DON: "We _____ _____ done that. _____ _____
(6)   (7)   (8)   (9)

see the construction in front _____ the entrance
(10)

_____ the street?"
(11)

SANDY: "What construction? If there had been any construction, I

_____ _____ seen it. It _____ _____ been
(12)   (13)   (14)   (15)

another street."

DON: "Well, never mind. I think we need _____ find a gas
(16)

station. There _____ _____ been one back there
(17)   (18)

somewhere."

57

SANDY: "There _____ _____ been one back a mile
                      (19)   (20)

_____ so."
      (21)

(10 Minutes Later)

GAS STATION ATTENDANT:

"_____ I help _____?"
          (22)   (23)

DON: "Yes. We're lost. I think we _____ _____ taken the
                                              (24)   (25)

wrong exit off the freeway. We're _____ for Lewis
                                                  (26)

Street."

ATTENDANT:

"_____ _____ _____ turned left on Clark
      (27)   (28)   (29)

Street. Then _____ _____ _____ seen Lewis
                    (30)   (31)   (32)

Street on _____ left."
                (33)

SANDY: "We _____ _____ driven right by it _____ not
                    (34)   (35)   (36)

seen it."

ATTENDANT:

"The street sign _____ _____ been down. That
                        (37)   (38)

happens during the rains. Anyway, take a right out

_____ the gas station. Go straight for a mile. Then turn
      (39)

left on Clark Street. Lewis Street will be on _____ left."
                                                        (40)

DON: "Thank you."

"to" after a vowel sound ———→ *da

NOTE: The reduced form ***da** is common after *go*. *To* is not pronounced ***da** if stressed.

PART I

Listen to the tape. You will hear the pairs of sentences listed below. The first sentence in each pair will be spoken with *careful pronunciation*. The second sentence will be spoken with *relaxed pronunciation*.

CAREFUL (SLOW) PRONUNCIATION	RELAXED (FAST) PRONUNCIATION
1. Where do you want to go?	1. Where do *ya *wanna go?
2. I want to go to Los Angeles.	2. I *wanna go *da Los Angeles.
3. And then?	3. *'N' then?
4. And then I'm going to try to go to San Diego.	4. *'N' then I'm *gonna try *da go *da San Diego.
5. What are you going to do if you go to San Diego?	5. *Whaddaya *gonna do if *ya go *da San Diego?
6. I'm going to go to the zoo.	6. I'm *gonna go *da the zoo.
7. Do you know how to get to the zoo when you're in San Diego?	7. Do *ya know how *da get *ta the zoo when *yer in San Diego?
8. No, I don't. Do *you* know how to get there?	8. No, I don't. Do *you* know how *da get there?
9. Sure. I know an easy way to get there. It's fast, too.	9. Sure. I know an easy way *da get there. It's fast, too.
10. Well, then, why don't you go to San Diego with me?	10. Well, then, why don't *cha go *da San Diego with me?

Close your book. Listen to the tape. You will hear the 10 sentences with relaxed pronunciation that you heard in Part I. After you hear each sentence, say the same thing, but use *careful pronunciation*.

PART III

Open your book. Listen to the tape. You will hear a conversation. In it, the speakers will use relaxed pronunciation. As you listen, fill in the blanks with the words you would hear if the speakers were using *careful pronunciation*. Replay the tape as necessary.

SIGHTSEEING

BEN: "Do _____ _____ _____
         (1)   (2)   (3)

_____ _____ Disneyland?"
   (4)   (5)

TAMMY: "Yes. I'd love _____ _____ _____ Disneyland.
                           (6)   (7)   (8)

What time do _____ _____ _____ try
                (9)   (10)   (11)

_____ leave?"
   (12)

BEN: "Well, we've _____ _____ leave before noon
                      (13)   (14)

_____ we'll hit a lot _____ traffic. Where do
   (15)   (16)

_____ _____ _____ _____ _____
   (17)   (18)   (19)   (20)   (21)

have dinner?"

TAMMY: "_____ _____ _____ say _____ _____
            (22)   (23)   (24)   (25)   (26)

dinner at Disneyland?"

BEN: "I _____ _____ . _____ _____ think it'll
           (27)   (28)   (29)   (30)

cost a lot _____ money _____ eat there?"
              (31)   (32)

TAMMY: "Maybe. But if it does, that's okay. How many times do we

get _____ _____ _____ Disneyland, anyway?"
       (33)   (34)   (35)

20

for ─────▶ *fer

NOTE: *For* does not become ***fer** when stressed.

PART I

Listen to the tape. You will hear the pairs of sentences listed below. The first sentence in each pair will be spoken with *careful pronunciation*. The second sentence will be spoken with *relaxed pronunciation*.

CAREFUL (SLOW) PRONUNCIATION	RELAXED (FAST) PRONUNCIATION
1. I'm looking for a car.	1. I'm *lookin' *fer a car.
2. Are you looking for a new car or a used one?	2. Are *ya *lookin' *fer a new car *er a used one?
3. For a used one.	3. *Fer a used one.
4. What year are you looking for?	4. What year are *ya *lookin' for?
5. I'm looking for a '78 or '79.	5. I'm *lookin' *fer a '78 *er '79.
6. How much do you want to spend for the car?	6. How much do *ya *wanna spend *fer the car?
7. What can I get for $500?	7. What *kin I get *fer $500?
8. Not much. But I have a 1978 Chevrolet I can give you for $1500.	8. Not much. But I have a 1978 Chevrolet I *kin give *ya *fer $1500.
9. What can I get for a thousand dollars?	9. What *kin I get *fer a thousand dollars?
10. Can you wait for a week? I think I'm going to have something in your price range then.	10. *Kin *ya wait *fer a week? I think I'm *gonna have something in *yer price range then.

PART II

Close your book. Listen to the tape. You will hear the 10 sentences with relaxed pronunciation that you heard in Part I. After you hear each sentence, say the same thing, but use *careful pronunciation*.

PART III

Open your book. Listen to the tape. You will hear a conversation. In it, the speakers will use relaxed pronunciation. As you listen, fill in the blanks with the words you would hear if the speakers were using *careful pronunciation*. Replay the tape as necessary.

THE PERFECT CAR

SALESMAN: "_____ (1) I help _____ (2)?"

JOHN: "Yes. I'm _____ (3) _____ (4) a used car."

SALESMAN: "What kind _____ (5) car are _____ (6) _____ (7) _____ (8)?"

JOHN: "I _____ (9) _____ (10) try _____ (11) find a late model economy car."

SALESMAN: "Say no more. I have the perfect car _____ (12) _____ (13). Follow me."

JOHN: "Is *this* it?"

SALESMAN: "This is the one. Isn't it beautiful?"

JOHN: "I _____ (14) _____ (15). The paint's chipped."

SALESMAN: "No problem. If _____ (16) pay a few dollars _____ (17) a paint job, it'll be as good as new."

JOHN: "How many miles has it got?"

SALESMAN: "Oh, around 95,000. But if _____ (18) pay a few dollars _____ (19) an overhaul, it'll be as good as new."

JOHN: "The tires _____ (20) _____ (21) be changed. They're bald."

SALESMAN: "_____ (22) right. But if _____ (23) pay a few dollars _____ (24) new tires, you'll have a beautiful car. Right? Right! Now _____ (25) _____ (26) _____ (27) say?"

ANSWER KEY

1. AT THE LAUNDROMAT (*ya):

1. you	2. you	3. you	4. you	5. you	6. You
7. You	8. you	9. you	10. you	11. you	12. you
13. you	14. you	15. you			

2. WEEKEND PLANS (*whaddaya):

1. What	2. are	3. you	4. What	5. do	6. you
7. What	8. do	9. you	10. you	11. What	12. do
13. What	14. do	15. you	16. What	17. do	18. You
19. What	20. do	21. you	22. What	23. do	

3. AT TOM'S FAST FOODS (*wanna):

1. What	2. do	3. you	4. want	5. to	6. want
7. to	8. What	9. do	10. you	11. want	12. to
13. want	14. to	15. want	16. to	17. you	

4. THE MONSTER THAT ATE CLEVELAND (*gonna):

1. What	2. are	3. you	4. going	5. to	6. going
7. to	8. you	9. want	10. to	11. What	12. are
13. you	14. going	15. to	16. want	17. to	18. you
19. going	20. to	21. going	22. to	23. you	24. you

5. DECISIONS, DECISIONS (*donno):

1. don't	2. know	3. What	4. do	5. you	6. don't
7. know	8. you	9. want	10. to	11. you	12. What
13. are	14. you	15. going	16. to	17. you	18. don't
19. know	20. want	21. to	22. don't	23. know	24. going
25. to	26. you	27. want	28. to	29. don't	30. know
31. What	32. do	33. you			

6. AT THE BUS STOP (*ta):

1. to	2. to	3. to	4. going	5. to	6. you
7. to	8. What	9. do	10. you	11. to	12. What
13. are	14. you	15. going	16. to	17. want	18. to
19. want	20. to	21. to	22. want	23. to	24. to
25. don't	26. know	27. going	28. to	29. to	30. to
31. to					

7. TO PULL OR NOT TO PULL (*gotta, *hafta, *hasta):

1. got	2. to	3. has	4. to	5. going	6. to
7. to	8. you	9. you	10. have	11. to	12. You
13. going	14. to	15. has	16. to	17. you	18. don't
19. know	20. has	21. to	22. to	23. have	24. to
25. to	26. to	27. got	28. to	29. have	30. to
31. have	32. to	33. to	34. got	35. to	36. got
37. to	38. has	39. to			

8. WEDDING BELLS (*yer, *yers):

1. your 2. your 3. your 4. going 5. to 6. to
7. you 8. don't 9. know 10. you 11. your 12. you
13. yours 14. What 15. do 16. you 17. your 18. have
19. to 20. You're 21. got 22. to 23. what 24. do
25. have 26. to 27. got 28. to 29. got 30. to
31. your 32. yours 33. your 34. going 35. to 36. have
37. to

9. LOOKING FOR AN APARTMENT (*cha, *cher):

1. want 2. you 3. to 4. you 5. what 6. you're
7. got 8. to 9. don't 10. you 11. to 12. you
13. What 14. you're 15. want 16. to 17. At 18. your
19. You're 20. going 21. to 22. want 23. to 24. aren't
25. you 26. don't 27. know 28. have 29. to 30. Don't
31. you 32. what 33. you're

10. SHOPPING (*-in'):

1. you 2. looking 3. you 4. want 5. to 6. looking
7. you 8. going 9. to 10. have 11. to 12. having
13. bending 14. don't 15. you 16. looking 17. you 18. you
19. taking 20. buying 21. you 22. You're 23. standing

11. GOING TO THE BARBER (*whacha):

1. What 2. are 3. you 4. doing 5. want 6. to
7. going 8. to 9. What 10. are 11. you 12. going
13. to 14. doing 15. going 16. to 17. What 18. do
19. you 20. want 21. to 22. Your 23. getting 24. what
25. you 26. What 27. are 28. you 29. going 30. to
31. you're 32. getting 33. your 34. having 35. what 36. you
37. your 38. don't 39. you 40. what 41. you 42. want
43. your 44. to 45. getting 46. What 47. you

12. FILL IT UP (*ja, *jer):

1. you 2. to 3. you 4. going 5. to 6. going
7. want 8. to 9. you 10. your 11. You're 12. you
13. your 14. You 15. to 16. you 17. don't 18. know
19. you 20. you 21. going 22. to 23. You 24. you
25. you 26. going 27. to

13. AT THE COFFEE SHOP (*er):

1. Would 2. you 3. to 4. or 5. you 6. want
7. to 8. got 9. to 10. to 11. you 12. want
13. to 14. or 15. or 16. to 17. don't 18. know
19. you 20. to 21. going 22. to 23. you 24. or
25. to 26. What 27. do 28. you 29. want 30. to
31. you 32. or 33. Would 34. you

14. AT THE POST OFFICE (*'e, *'is, *'im, *'er, *'em):

1. want 2. to 3. to 4. you 5. want 6. to
7. them 8. sending 9. them 10. to 11. have 12. to
13. them 14. him 15. What 16. do 17. you 18. don't
19. know 20. to 21. her 22. her 23. have 24. to
25. to 26. he 27. has 28. to 29. them 30. her
31. her 32. them 33. him 34. or 35. them 36. to
37. your 38. he 39. them 40. his 41. him 42. he
43. them 44. his 45. he 46. his

15. TAXI, TAXI (*'n'):

1. and	2. want	3. to	4. starving	5. going	6. to
7. and	8. your	9. them	10. and	11. them	12. What
13. do	14. you	15. him	16. don't	17. know	18. and
19. and	20. get	21. your	22. your	23. and	

16. THE ROCK CONCERT (*kin):

1. Can	2. you	3. did	4. you	5. Can	6. you
7. can	8. Don't	9. you	10. Can	11. you	12. Don't
13. you	14. them	15. Can	16. you	17. to	18. Can
19. you	20. you	21. coming	22. have	23. to	24. to
25. can	26. you				

17. AT THE SUPERMARKET (*a):

1. of	2. of	3. and	4. of	5. Can	6. you
7. of	8. of	9. to	10. of	11. Can	12. you
13. of	14. got	15. to	16. going	17. or	18. going
19. to	20. of	21. coming	22. to		

18. GETTING DIRECTIONS (*shoulda, *coulda, *woulda, *musta, *maya, *mighta):

1. What	2. do	3. you	4. should	5. have	6. couldn't
7. have	8. Didn't	9. you	10. of	11. to	12. would
13. have	14. must	15. have	16. to	17. must	18. have
19. might	20. have	21. or	22. Can	23. you	24. may
25. have	26. looking	27. You	28. should	29. have	30. you
31. would	32. have	33. your	34. must	35. have	36. and
37. might	38. have	39. of	40. your		

19. SIGHTSEEING (*da):

1. you	2. want	3. to	4. go	5. to	6. to
7. go	8. to	9. you	10. want	11. to	12. to
13. got	14. to	15. or	16. of	17. you	18. want
19. to	20. go	21. to	22. What	23. do	24. you
25. to	26. having	27. don't	28. know	29. Don't	30. you
31. of	32. to	33. to	34. go	35. to	

20. THE PERFECT CAR (*fer):

1. Can	2. you	3. looking	4. for	5. of	6. you
7. looking	8. for	9. want	10. to	11. to	12. for
13. you	14. don't	15. know	16. you	17. for	18. you
19. for	20. have	21. to	22. You're	23. you	24. for
25. what	26. do	27. you			